Eye of the Spiral

James Grabill

Eye of the Spiral
Copyright © 2022 by James Grabill

Cover Art:

James Grabill
Eye of the Spiral

Back Cover Portrait: *Bill Siverly*

Book Design by:

UnCollected Press
8320 Main Street, 2nd Floor
Ellicott City, MD 21043

For more books by UnCollected Press:
www.therawartreview.com

First Edition 2022
ISBN: 978-1-7378731-7-4

Contents – Eye of the Spiral

III.

We are entering a new era, one of rapid and often unpredictable climate change. In fact, the new climate norm is change. Many resources are becoming scarce but none more scarce than time.　**— Lester Brown**

The new, visionary civilization must arise out of masses of people tapping some basic human core of resonance with the underlying potentials in nature, but in a way in which they maintain open access to it.　**— Lorin Hollander**

We aren't separate from this planet; we are part of this planet. Our minds may think that we are humans, that those are animals, and those are plants, but I think many of us have come to think that we're all part of one.
—Paul Stamets

It is very rare for a being to take human form.
— V.V. Kalu Rinpoche

I.

IN THE GLOW OF THE RIVER

Maybe we've seen ourselves overhead
in the night sky streaking unexpectedly
through the universe in the tail end
of a comet sputtering and popping
as a miner's fuse burning down faster
to the motherload the longer we think
the more time that goes past drowning
in meteor showers over the insect prairies
penetrating the troposphere to unsheath
crocosmia on the ground of evidence
with leaves that reveal mathematics
of the plotted Mandelbrot number series
in their design surfacing out of the genome
going eye to eye, cells to cells, at the foot
of the heights that were cleared for spider
roads strung up between things that remain
firm with their Aztec plazas dreaming fast
holding plumb under auspices saddened
semi-sweet with whistling of the hungrier
trucks burning into town through bilges
of summer in the little swallows of tree frogs
croaking out purrs in the glow off the river
passing the house forever under starlight.

OUT OF THE GREEN

Green plants punch out of the unnamed soil
at ragged edges of sky-burned mountain-top
coal peppering the recent incomplete history
of a few thousand incompatible religious sects,

each referring to their muskellunge doctrines
swimming in cold pools along the lake bottom
of gamma-ray magnitudes, in the up-birded
and heavy present place where we were born.

It's the aftermath of 1960s antiwar protests
beneath the sky's glistering million billions
widening catalytic pressures on slow-motion
fall of the sun along the curve of cheekbones.

What pushes undergoes plunges and breeches,
grails, granges, sprawls, eucalyptus and soils
at the root of deciding system cells, absorbing
brightness mollified by innocence as by the rain.

The presence of trees holds species in the future
limits of shape, as what we've known approaches
an event horizon beyond which nothing escapes,
nothing alive, no name nailed up along the road.

Only after this morning's swallowed countless
galaxies and suns out of unending night sky,
20th century cannonball lanterns still burning,
a green dragonfly slips out of a break in the air.

AROUND LIGHT

The sky rounds off,
around capillary draw
into architectural
columns sea-spun
out of mushroom licks
in soil delivering mineral
mid-afternoon in another person
and another, on out, all holding
and held by the sluice and pitch
of moss-green simultaneous assumptions,
in the dark and light knot parked here
as matter tendering curves one with another,
the different and same spun here, torn
as from indivisible meridians arced taut.
For each calculated point centers the way it is,
complexity tying down what's going to be needed,
say by Samson laboring to hold up an executive
office and atrium with varied counterbalances
of planetary drive behind the hammered bronze
mask of Venus worn by those heaving with grief
for other animals in the long-range forest echo
from before massive thinking managed to
centralize, dispersed as it's been within
collaborating cells with leaf veins hungry
for gravity from unobtainable photobarometric
slopes burying imprints of ribs, as transpiration
releases the next showering blue multiples,
sea lions in rock-sled crawls, oysters cradled
in spits, oceans undulating musculature,
sunlight rippling over the white genetic horses
of noon, with mycelial reaches that continue
as if meaning still had a hand open in this
long French film three months and counting,
rolling on between aeronautical years of any
soothsaid 2020s splashing down around bends
where archaic mammalian ancestors have been

located with the first unconditional mother
baked up by bodily cells converging in mind,
upright arousal powered by extended viscera
and otherwise undetectable shuck around each
parachuting haul of breath and magnanimous
filling human chest carried by wide shoulders
of sleep and back-lit underwater slowness,
the infra-radiant speeds suspended in amoebic
rotations as turn looming weave, nautilus spiral
compounding before hundred-year suns
congregate and collide in confluent pulses
of the onrush toward knowing as offshore
forests of kelp shield tiniest solar eggs glued
to the crab-claw bottom of blameless mind
in wind rippling orchards out of the rock
and deep-whale glide as if bees weren't gone
and ashes of newly cut forests hadn't turned
translucent with modern vulnerability,
spreading light over breakers as crush
grains remaking them, returning
what's silken and buoyant, swimming
with weight of so many asleep or awake
in the moment wide waves circulate
cellular shape through the feel
of presence deciding on a feather.

WHERE THE NEXT WAVE HAS BEEN

As the greased axle keeps turning the galaxy,
it rolls out capillary lifts and lengthy heaves
of unfinished work and contagious bearing.
Contemporary but ancient flowerheads bend
toward Earth, to where the place rounds off,
restored by unfolding spiral ratios within cells.

So cool fiddleneck ferns in their bowl of light
unroll Stradivarius necks plumb, breathing
out through vibratory underground mists.
Where the breaking wave has been—will be
everything living or not that touched it off.
Pacific rain and archaic rock uncoil in a snail
shell from far back. The vulnerable wall of sleep,
heat-trapping sense in common, shows through
long-term breakthrough moves of mammal body,
the pulse of small humming wings athletic as fresh
grains of brown rice, prismatic at unleveling heights.

Spreads and contractions of individuals turn up
over hundreds of miles, as the sky wheels past
the edge of current resistance to the inevitable
as the unknown leaches out of the unconscious
into love or fear. We can see what home is,
how being can be, that it's something shared
with the formidable trees that keep us alive.

OUT OF THE QUICK

If you're sleeping while long distance rings up all night,
fog horns moaning, packed unconscious cloud cover
drifting past dry with soot-bedocked psychokinetic yes
and no that nevertheless rely on pollination, this era

when drought late in the afternoon descends on fields
or 100-year floods suddenly break with the continuum,

know that the compass core revolves on the living root,
whatever's become moth-vanished, as long or as short
as anyone's firsts or lasts torched along with the rectitude
in leaves. Where muscular phenomena tough to perceive
continue, they may be found or lost in paranormal sinks

of ferocious North American limbo, where misinformation
campaigns trying to starve "the other" impact their own,

and by undertaking blanket assaults on the community
threaten what their own kids depend on, by forcing
austerity on citizens in the history of biblical exploits.

So more untoward dusts shower anyone's greater or lesser
daily strife, with transmutations of indignity powering up
when summer's laying down more pavement from before
what matters, in what the seeds carry out with cellular lift.

Of course, the blue sky exists, but is it the same presence
that inspired the honest longer-term light in civilization?

While comprehension operates in the back-roar, the winds
turn massive global turbines, ringing with electromagnetic
desire over loose pack of the clay always swallowing treason
with loyalty, as severity crystalizes in the vaults of poverty.

BLUE SCARF

Long hair falls onto shoulders in a future impossible to imagine.

The coyote circles back behind languages of other species, where *The Book of Tenderness* is still being written into the cells.

The fruit of apple takes shape around its seed.

The root wheel turns, ground-feeding jays and dog-dreaming morning, launching the blue scarf in the sky.

The lit candle flies parallel to the world.

In moth-vanished hammerings, the diesel locomotive thunders.

Ancestry starts within animal silence.

Poplars rake through future breath.

THIS

Before dawn cracked out of its hen's egg,
we had the bottom line of divine decree.

We had the next world vaguely planned out.
We sensed bad luck originated with being bad.

We learned that destiny hinged on cosmic judgment
that came down hard in life, and harder in death.

Before dawn, someone stood at the horizon,
a future man or woman looking back at us,

at the god-damned dumb of us that we carry
around as evidence we were little once

and, in fact, infants, if you're willing
to go back far enough, to the beginning.

And yet dawn happened, with consciousness
born as a process, ongoing and unfinished

with growth, while providing us with peaks
as if everything behind us had led up to this.

AT THE ROOT OF NERVE

The raucous crows carry on, mothering the young,
passing along crow wisdom, managing a few places
in the heights. What's unfinished, we understand,
can be beautiful, where the Hubble has revealed
before our eyes distant alien birth clouds of suns,
over caws where the crows are mothering the ground.
Where the spectrum's broken into individual greens
and red-violets back in the embassies of old trees
handling the heaviness of our own moth-wing future
with honesty that's theirs. In the practice of waking
and sleeping, rhizomes sweeten after a spring rain
when wood smoke's blessing, spoiling, and marking
the air. Doesn't temporal intensity splinter unfinished
in microseconds wielding stained-glass preexistence
through unpainted back doors? Whatever has been
mothering the common ground, haven't we failed
to live this life, and haven't we succeeded? Isn't this
a chance before unpredictable weather breaks into hot
and cold? With downpours of solar light driving wheat
made out of planetary orbiting, what comes of talk
grows present, with unfinished rooms on the house.

ENCIRCLING LOOM

Amniotic drops of prehistoric dew on the canyon rim walls luminesce with light in the brain.

Complex otherness floats in womb-pulse swaths crossing the Pacific in adaptations of bodily cells.

Under blinding stars, electrical ancestral stories pour down through the small houses of losses and gain, where future scarcity looms and a dark-violet eyelash carries more weight than we know.

As the road goes out on its own, the root in a seed will decide. Where daylight drives the atmosphere, a shirtless boy swims in the sea of air. The cradle collides with shadow and magnetic lineage in current encircling turns.

As overflow sleep expands and contacts in the spectrum, the unfinished complex mind has an eye for complexity in the world.

Isn't this where separation from the whole grew opposable thumbs and set off on the road coming back?

What part of the whole would being exclude? What animals haven't loved and feared this air?

FLUID RIPS IN THE FABRIC

However the first wheel began to work with bulk inclination
however many ancestors were granted clearance to speak
at the same hallucinatory moment of quiet, inhaling, whaling
or looking off to this day back when it was still only a little risk

in the mammoth history of chance and success
ensconced in what may have been rough
or prismatic in the face of lamp-quick qualms
fresh as spoons of air at pungent end-lands with hungers
like ours and our lineages of case studies pushed ahead
into unusual attempts not to end before finishing or going
indivisible from sea-slogged risks in colt-thick chances
the carrying capacity of this planet may have in it

where the mind pictures what it used to think
would be ahead of whatever taste it once had
of primordial air that planted its taproot in being
where mercy cultures have had their equivalencies
and inequities conjured up in the sun that quickens
down to sleep within history eventually
the way unfathomed antiquity resounds

where, awake or falling asleep, the deep brain works
on its own, as the mind is only one human
center of activity in the whole which is far more
than mind in the domain of matter sweetening
in elastic time as core-spun seedlings
respond in the keeping of kindred night

the shadow canyon at noon translucent at cellular times
of birth depth-sounded through churns of exotic torque
in public plants out of speech at the root-core in bone-making
to drive the room of summer out to indigenous parallels
in front-line questioning of the black umbrella under satellites
in heavily patented identity, for the next generations will
have their needs and demands other than any
known at this point of intrinsic worth this instant
in night-to-night expansions of molecular integrity
as if what can you do with undercurrents in the original

nuts and screws of uncontested accelerations of simplicity
sleep-raked as silence nailed by motel neon into vastness
as if nothing's happened for decades, before it shows up
with glass ceilings or rail-yard lanterns of unusual
psychic beauty in the truck and delivery of burden

from the first birth going anywhere in this wind-soaked
mattering where the world's said to be riding buoyancy
in gravity for miles that thicken and thin in their soups
coming to live in dimension, talking their sun's medicine
and sea-tortoise tympanum, however the place looks
through these eyes when no one could know
who was going to be taking this breath
someplace other than where we've been

adorned by genetic necklaces of forest intelligence
or swelling in seamless saws from the burn
at absolute zero, the forward comb out of starts
of embryonic depth, the undefined heaviness
and lightening from the sky-down south honeybees
that chance their root-reaching hexagonal symmetry
on the only breath we have and use in poor villages
on the wrists of river thunderheads, vector songbirds

breathing the daylight air, packed as it's been
with night locomotives that blow in from work
sweats and animals out shuddering in the collective
sense written in uberclavicular pretexts of onion stands
say, green as the scarlet rock of hips pressing on
with subsensory pulse, in professional detachment

when the green wave crashes, exceeding expectation
which awaits or dissolves with the laying on of flat-past
visceral intensifications of hands as revolve around oil
in an era of belief in belongings, which lionizes control
of whatever grows or might be the effect of a root
drawn into what it needs and can give back to soils.

HIERONYMUS BOSCH RINGS THE CALDRON BELL SPILLING OUT MORE FARM HANDS

In lamp-quick hulk uphammering depths
and black iris lulls out of nowhere
as from a dream of your unexpected wedding
on the sea floor, where sumac-crimson crown jewels
and thick golden rings of archbishops only end up
darker and more glowing than words we might have
around spaghetti-strapped aching summer
with mile-long shadows of 21st century rainwater-slept
trepidations half-shot and staff-stalked before
heading north at night, where they're already
plucking the chicken string harp of starlight,
until dawn happens to be filling in, rounding off
space for vanishing animals from its seat in molecular
integrity, as we've found in long sweeps of beseeming
that, lacking a name, may have gone unseen
before anyone's embryonic tortoise-crawl personage
could be wheeling in prehistoric tundra bubbling
methane into the first air around blank-slate innocence
at Celsius-laden extremes of the appetites, spill-spaced,
baked into feasting or fasting under radiographic displays
of leaves decrying their latest report of what's known
or has crowded into the sun's mouth as pilots a sweet
bent into this moment and the next, then further,
launching reasonable attempts to outwit any incendiary
doubt with unattempted thought of the long-term
coal-smoldering past as cauldron workers on break
in spring-offs of lineage which begin in crawls
before knuckling under vacuum-soaked roars
at the lip of disappearing descended from the Dust
Bowl, going, going, and then gone unremembered
as social or riverous before broilers or displays
of propulsion out of the most unnatural
current of row-shouldered hithers herded unbled
and kicking, over free-floating Viking burials as reside
in a flaming fortune out of the light-thundered origin
streaming with torque building up at sea-flood barriers
with overpeopled edges of massive under-governed
chemistries in fits of billionaire post-hypnotic

19

suggestion storming up with what was a little quick
dispersion falling into pockets of openness
birds have left behind, where hundreds of colonized
years must surrender to genetic code lighting itself
such scarlet sky as never could be named
after somebody we know, as a lumber crew
has been dreaming the grain in forest floors close
to further neighborhood houses sliding down
more from the clouds and lone fish-swim lows
to the mineral night-but-day heights now at risk
over coffins in the rocky hills rocking kings down
to the middle of Earth in the medieval bell tower
not even burning with what the sun's ignited
where mammalian mammoth afternoon genes
transom from coolingness and detonations of high
noon give nano-birth to an inconsolable defense
vulnerability industry around which charging
bullet-packed pork-barreled incentives churn
up further war, with scarf-bonneted crones
of the more operatic traditions climbing
down to the barnyard from a drenched tulip
the size of a medieval village cooking vat
just to leave sunlight a little kiss
on the side of the neck before falling
back on such billowing Hieronymus
Bosch hinds, as demonstrate how
the time's been wide but largely unclear
how long it may have, given its forest
necklaces still with a muscular chance
to kneel before anyone's mask-head
spreads with infra-fossiled beseeming
just sheepherding off in them yonders
as zinc-forward in manifest Bosch
able to pony up alongside
what once dewlap-split
with the bawling whole.

ASTROLOGIA

Earth circles around the sun, with suddenly blue
Ford Galaxies packing hydraulics of the jet sky,
the cricket pulse within the bones making us blood,
enough to monetarily fill with silver rain flushed
down re-history. Doll eyes following a dollar around
in the white room trail oversee Supreme Court rulings
in Florida. Dark-gray tenements withhold great gravity
for the living who prosper by who knows how it was
going to be, when never have we had another time
more than this time now.
                                    People climb into a packed
city bus, as manifest car lights trowel for redemption.
Engines submerged in moving muffle certain fallings
into the open, particular expoundings, delicate exhales.
The heart-beating unknown evening might as well grant
plenty of time, where we're everything the moon has lit,

while the doctored reverend coos into an ear of the baby
of self-imposed sanctions. As a woman's sweeping atoms
into a corner of her spectroscopic addition, she discovers
parts of many in the one she knows she's driving through
gravitationally, in up-heard pitches, with cities now seen
from the shuttle, Hubble receivers in resilient amber waves
heightening the body of a tree the body knows pretty clearly.

All the world is how you've given it a place around you.
All you can do is how time opens and closes as you work
by the scent of long hair, of dusty blackberries, bitter cigar,
violet scarf, the steel frame shuddering as we slow--a taste
of sudden ginger with phantom old-world willows rustling,
with heavy shepherding of suitcoats for a slowest particle,
rainwater outside and in, wild passing light—continually
the human face being born.
                                    Therefore, cleverness wraps us
with outer ancestor space, as green plants grow, spinning
out of genes as the cross-modified sky galaxy groundingly
revolves, matter drinking root light. Nothing can be done
that isn't trying and letting go, the whole-housed nuclear
flashes emulsified instantly gone. The ocean coast talks
about it better than words. It depends on your inner sun.

from **Double Helix**

It is good to remember that the laws of the universe recognize no favorites and cherish no hostility or small vindictiveness, that before sun and rain, stormy winds, or summer's kind beneficence, we all stand upon one common level.
— **Caroline Henderson**, *Letters from the Dust Bowl*

✳

We're looking at light of rain forest moss,
beetles no one has seen, brief flashes
of estuary fish swimming undiscovered

miles through symphonic thermonuclear truce

within the sky, leaving the night open
sanctuary merging on Bangkok streets echoing

Peruvian flutes, spaghetti-strapped Hungarian
accents of whole wheat current from new solar
thermal towers, buildings which have slid through
numerals from Mayan charts, indicating a galaxy

spine in new arcing multiples of ten, as rough
streetlight glisters raw from sterling silver octane,
with uncertain consequences in a glass of tap water

as encyclopedic in chemistry as human hunger,

as elegant prehistoric amber necklaces, as old-growth
forest intelligence giving a single cell ethical accord,

how do you say, where the calm center begins

when what you do and what goes on hold honest
shares of the unseen, for man with his white shirts
and first petitions of dust and deployment of arms
and neck, the shoulders and forehead with its ability

to sense immensity, down to the nails carpenters use
for a place to stay next to iridescent breathing beauty,

engrained with desire not so much for meals of meat
as fruit, not so much ancient drums but how a brain
can use its peak oceanic sadness to see the hour of birth

is ancient, as if we've been one another, the stone house
with the sense it has a spiral tower where someone
is asking not only what might be easy to picture
after being reminded of it by the body moving through

other species, as if we'd just found ourselves waking

Tibetan with so many still in shock from their own
births, the naked force placing the body on steel
medical tables, the first merging gone into attempts

to breathe, out of desperation in daytime rooms
of the story, shoulders soothed by summer rain,
walls of old books on intuitive kinesis as a work crew

has been reconstructing long-held assumptions
across that yard in snapshots understandable

as current extending the range of sudden parallel,

as ongoing as amendments to soil still working
and reverberating cells that will chord up a place
to be accordingly, with apples when they're ripening,

where we may or may not be living out our lives.

✱

What has already broken
off from usefulness
whirls up in yellow-gold marigold
pollen floating over North
American nightcrawlers glistening
with mud of feather fiber and eggshell
mayfly carcasses, the cross-mingled
lichen and white hair with molecules
in jurisdictions of the unseen,

the disintegrated baby cough
fresh water, the shaken-off
heavy museums of violet outskirts,

the root of sense at the ground
of the world, honey bees imprinted
on origin, peppering of tribal

calculus on road signs every so
often, the downsized next place
with mile-high crow wing
open-bloomed night sky.

Through exhalations, prejudicial
appeals the hour makes
have their blue jay feathers

that grow along nerve
as the young maple has spread
branches more apart in the blue

bowl of unfinished hours
that make room in back

so the flowering ovum
turns into sweetness.

✸

Underground pressures, sunlight
shattering sharp on the fractures,
with sunken linkage, spools of arc

grazing out restless, complex, panscopic,
harboring elevations
of the invisible up-rocked stallion

or hypnotisms living in bacterial swims
open personally along shoulders
the eyes have for a road
under unretouched melting

the crawling and recasting of rain, the long

day gone into crops
as yellow-amber
into feathers, blue along spreads

within brilliant silver-black
as you've called the night in yourself
and answered with quiet
breaking mesa solitude out

until flying the first ambient, vibratory

hours above what longing has
this time, the sun, birth,
the tens of millions the moment
before mastodons painted themselves

with flank shouldering bones
of the night sky
into the ground, concentric
along verges and soft

with the numbers of brown.

✳

Before bugling, a regular male elk

will borrow the lungs of green trees
and tilt his head back, the heavy antlers
aiming him at star clusters. He'll let it fly

out in a cloud of steam, the high squeal,
arcing from the forces of elk past
and future, where he is, how ready he is,
delivering it far into the sky, as his cry
calls and breaks into silent clearings
to stands of the night, being elk, arcing
out through night and waking her

out of her sleep, the whine firing straight
into her mind, from his core, past any
clenched jaw from chest-barreled ancestral
elk he must feel, when you've got to know
weight on your head is being sent far,
before it showers into the clearing

where she's awake, to the flying-in song
of breath steaming, longing through
moon with its steady light among so many
needles of fir, the long cry of fire-lit cells
of lungs, from one into the immensity

of another, from one ancestral bearing
you can't hold back, so you tilt your head
using the exquisite powerful neck,
spreading the teeth apart to send it,
becoming it, flying out into dark
where you're home, where you're home
with ancestors in your cells sounding
through you and yet only you are

calling for her from the blood and weight,
the past lifting out of the ground, rising
into you and bursting out through
your throat into the wild future of elk.

✺

Good reasons exist on Earth
to shield the mind from hope
we've lost, given what's at risk.

But in evening air by the river,
what the eyes see of the city
on the banks a little way off
the ears pick up in river waves.
The fertile scent is of water
and topsoil that a root needs.

From across the water, voices
of children almost reach us,
but already they've headed off
into a future that survives us.

They're playing, growing into lives
as if there were no question
ancestors hadn't once faced,
as if the readiness built in
to the body over eons were right.

In the middle of this, hope
isn't necessary and loss
of hope nothing they'll hear.

They've imprinted on conditions
into which they were born
believing all this is the world.

✸

Strings that continue to reverberate in the wake of bow

iron above ground, animal heads on sails, sensorium of cells,
the solemn red-center carriage of self induced by night sky,

the yellowing material bake at knifepoint prow exempting no one,
the red-violet neon beats of drum, as flash through neural timber,

the shadow density in bioaccumulative tinctures of the absolute
in prime colors, as sweeten loom, ovum and the billion perfumes,

Peruvian peak meditations in sadness over the incomplete distance,
the heaving swells of baking future bread with people almost heard,

arsenic from mines, loss of bees, bleached coral, methane thaws,
the scarlet-dark landfill leachate burning down to buried rains,

apocalyptic belief, and faceless soil going to town on everyone else,

the heights of rock, bends, blood and swaying as the wind has gone,

triclosan-dieldrin weaves in a place walking on curves,

the electrical plants ushering hungers along into the future of cells.

✹

An ant's duty beneath the night
sky vastness, given the hunger
on the ground, has been to tend
the mother who carries on the inheritance
selected of their labors and the touch
they have with the nectar of fallen leaves,

delivering generations to the future
that remains unknown, down there
in the looming underground old ocean
sands alive with foragers, crawlers,
and ant-cow aphids, with jumpers
and swimmers through undersoils,
and pushing burst-pouch intestinal
worms and scramblers tilling the place

from within. As the falcon flies in the open
air already starting to go, ants will continue
to work on unraveling what might have been
smothered, drawn as they are
to the country and cities showing
signs from before the place was

emptying itself out, to be filled again,
where the ancestors are, in soil
translating more glass shadows
in private landings of the moment
coming to a stop, rocking in place
with forages through corn-splashed
dusts with a half life that curls
and peels from the sky
into pieces of the forgotten,

which the ants take down
into aching that went under,
however many teachings
have been lost within
wing-beat impermanence.

✴

While the lengthy faithful
mineral satellites orbit
with their reading power,
the more thorny blackberry
vines burst apart
the ground in back,

under the invisible stars
of disciplines and modern
pungency of dropped
needles dips as it passes
the houses in time,

where not as many seem
practiced on their clavichords
or willing to put up
with complex consistency,
as absent and present
as summer momentum is,

when future dancers dive
then lower their long arcing
arms stirring the air with fiery
vestment, when drummers start
into miles of talking chest
carried by calm, before a fir
tree through limbs is releasing
archival golden camera flashes
in 1953 finding immeasurable
new surroundings, as all around,

matter is being, then being is
replaced by other matter
in what little we might know,
once something hard to hold
long enough for words
has been reaching closer
to old-world tables
of ancestral beauty.

＊

Possibility at the end
of "A Day in the Life"
from *Sgt. Pepper* converges

and peaks as the pitch slides higher
and then higher still, extending
through harmonic intermolecular
architecture, propagation of fingertip
transfer, the foundational electrification
through guitars into neurochemical leads

as ride the slow swaying walk, entrusting
indigenous findings to senses of the animal
that carries being through the world.

Maybe we're sensing a split-second river
of determinism altered by sharpness
or scent, say, of hair, or sense of being
at home, where the head is cradled for sleep,

as genetic gyre revolves around equal
interconnected gyre co-creating energy,
inclination, and cellular body, the electrical

star-spike melts of tundra sending out
and receiving long currents of flux,
centering inner centriole sun,
where the primal is conducted

back to the stone furnace fired up
at the bottom of the skeletal stairs,

while the brain dreams a person up
into capacity, whatever the species,
however unknown the future may be.

II.

Any person who loves another person,
Wherever in the world, is with us in this room –

— Kenneth Patchen

A CHAR SCENT IN THE AIR

Wildfires explode up slopes
crawling toward granges
in small foothills townships
where belief in the climate
has meant forgetting it.
The brain keeps revising
its scripts but could use more
time to catch up at the root
of what we are to the discovery of oil.
Meanwhile, transnational gas binges
have promulgated a big idea
that at first, for the ancients,
must have been a huge sensation,
that the god-like cosmic sun
orbits singularity of the human head.
Wherever it goes, filthy-rich oil
exacerbates cognitive dissonance
around its effects, while planting
its yard in steamrolled asphalt
lined with dancing-girl lounges.
Crude oil appears to understand
you can't know what you have
until a few billionaires are taking
all they can grab for their own.
Could someone explain how long
ungovernable salvation has
been hanging out in the museum
of train wrecks? The scent of char
outside today appears in the sad
story of a few astronomical
accounts with their poles
melting into oceans that look
away if someone's talking.

THE BRAIN TAKES ITS TIME

(Getting Around to Climate Change)

The brain takes its basement stairs
that lead down below the neighborhood,
where it's taking its time, hunting
through decades of *National Geographic*
for the rhinoceros of early parts of the last
century that lived out its life thrashing
through tall grasses of peace, an oxpecker
riding its ancient shoulders, ready
to whistle out an alarm if it sees a predator,
living on ticks and sips of blood if it can
find a wound. What's a little blood loss,
if a little surveillance wouldn't hurt the effort
around the wilder creations forced to hold
their own in unequivocal displays of prowess
in a place packed with crawling creeping
creatures that spread enzymes on pupae
before exploring forages or facing an enemy?
While the electrical brain works to finish
its chores, cleaning up dried-out brushes
and house paint cans, it digs into the garden,
working soil loose a moment in winds
from the papal palace that carry some away
with candle flashes of medieval armor
over mammoth affection the brain has had
for instinctive wherewithal in the smooth
feel of the body with regard for a hair's
or a city's width, around so much beauty
in nature and so much we've made
that immediately needs to be retooled.

ALL MORNING THE CLIMATE INCREASINGLY TURNS

With every cell tied to what hopes in a molecule, this present era of remote consequences shows how every bite appears to be taking it out on the wilderness.

Whether wisdom bites at your boot heels or the planet keeps going behind red curtains in the embassy of opposites, the baroque wheeling of air and water around Earth, as oceanic and precise as it may be, has been archaic and yet modern as morning skin.

With hypnotized angers going about bamboozling political will of the masses, morning sinks its silver spoon into the next roar of winds and squealing apparatus of eighteenth century assumptions no one's dismantled.

So who knows the exact month, season, and hour divine intent kicks in, cleaning the place up after us? In our freedom, who among us hasn't been owned by more than her own desire, more than inflations of rains that feather off the more serious melts in our saucering galaxy?

Morning light continues to shatter into spreads of color in parallel with the ancestral mind, as tongues are unconditional animals mostly before words, when isn't it time to admit that little exists other than what's here?

Wouldn't you say a clear and present threat to the population been the population? Hasn't all night through the day been where Northwest firs are risking their limbs?

But morning shouldn't be asking us much, even when all that exists plays the genetic keyboard before a fair share of bystanders and numerous public displays of impermanence.

IRREVERSIBLE SENSE

I.

Out of the smallest light-strike
tinctures of midnight
and dawn on the barges,

out of preconditional capture and release
of the atmosphere bearing down
on pilgrimages in the era before belief
in evolutionary intelligence of cells

where time has been the water
and mineral urgency progresses
more slowly than telephone-sky cameras
or an unprecedented word for *critical*
emerging from cell-to-cell kindred

at the root of being in a life,
improvised, out of being alive
as one among many, not many

with a whole lot of money of the grasses
under distant fields of the cumulative
stars in heavy revolution, leaving
in their wake the original dust
that even now circles the planet

as almost an endless number of sounds
in a voice, encompassing each possible
picture, yet every one preternatural,

every longing and conscious
sense, each further person born,
new to the planets circling the sun.

II.

The tin drum under seismic pressure
compresses into a little bell
still ringing in the underground home
where ants are running their big cities
at the edge of an asking root hair

down in soil which is packed with being,
where mineral exchanges happen fast
on slopes of concussive gravity
shaping emptiness within the bowl
which has never stopped working
since it was made by exploding methane
released in the middle of thawing tundra

the bowl that promises an answer to hunger,
the bowl created to hold what's in it,
what's dropped into it without breaking it
like almost every ancient Mayan bowl
with circumferential lips of pi
revolving with the equator
that encompasses what's adapted

the way the flower of the tree
turns over weeks into fruit
on the last branches to appear

before the face absorbed by air
can hear the sounds within voices
that communicate between species.

WE MUST ADAPT

Solar immensities in leaves and microflora have, of course, kept human hunger alive. Seven billion are quickly becoming eight, then nine approaching ten around 2050, unless hunger sets us back.

Each of us has similar needs, and at least archaic mothers in common, though we forget.

Through the lift or fall of electric nerve, root threads under slow-motion bearing of one to the next, the scarlet *no return* of philosophical doors, collisions have been written across the face of the sun—

The wall of sleep suffers from burst-horse coal.

Admiral teeth decorate the uniform ocean floor.

Torches pave a wingspan path from birth.

Affinity, unfinished, undergoes the longer term.

Emily Carr's inexorable day-lit spiraling galaxies turn through principalities in sea-bellowed blameless wind.

Where so many bodies wake or sleep, fresh loaves bake within genetic code. The double helix resonates into a next generation as the heat slides species out of sync, and how much hunger can the planet carry?

SHE EXPANDS AND CONTRACTS
WITH CONSCIOUSNESS

Her day-to-day future's framed
by the self-organized collective.
Her summer night has its crickets
sawing steadily through the floor
of self-importance as the brainstem
has been ecologically employed.
She flies into slipstreams, maneuvers
out of ancient painted mazes,
and is still drawn down Broadway
half-expecting to see her father.
Her mammoth northern glacier
may be unfreezing before us forever.
She sleeps where little now could
change the present now our past.
Her grip of ethical bearing soon gave
rise to a more refined fingertip touch.
She separates from the collective
before demonstrating her identity
at the bottom of the Grand Canyon
slathered over with midnight stars.
Her chanting calls on old masters
who discovered time to sit here,
as she's planted ends of her guitar
strings in soil with the pole beans.
Her cells borrow the matter they use
when transcending ownership.
The final bell before resounding dawn
has for many months asked for her
hand while she couples with remote
galaxies over the Madonna and Child.

SHE THRIVES ON CIRCULATION OF RAIN

In sunburst swells, her temptations unfold into insinuations
of cheek bones and the fine reception of seed corn in topsoil.
Her hydrostatic exotica superconduct sips of public water.
She weathers sense, burning incense, with a real sweet chance
of compromise with incompleteness through global circulation,
while days within days orbit on frequencies yet to be tuned in.
In her documentary film, each scene is a film in a film in a film.
In a locomotive spread, her massive whale dives, huge face first,
instantly adapting to the weight of the seas built up in hunger.
She repairs daily at a rate of hundreds of tons a microsecond.
Her flourishing pulse plants *no return* in low clouds off the
river. She refuses to quote forecasts that ignore weather in the
future where bridges have kept melting over the canyon of
flames, where the loudest cry can be the least heard and
mothers are whispering, *Take heart in the scent of Earth after
summer rain.*

HOWEVER MANY

However many names are written on doors,
however many sad melts of cathedrals
of ice, however spontaneous the blue is
in a person who refuses to consider the current
unknowns, whatever starlight tattoos in the summer
lull, in the half-future tombs where bones lie
badly, in the keep of a dozen million hooves
on the rock and furious slides on a fault,
the stabs of hunger off the tables, however likely
the cells are to re-establish readiness after disruption,
or dusk is liable to break in the wave of flux
or germinated shifts of double helix, resulting
in cultures of aversion to the immediate, however
many still-rumbling undercurrent heaves
hammer in a downpour, whoever may be walking
around, denying their own earthworm innards
or necessary number of mothers and fathers,
however developed the language seems,
however many compulsive reactions to the future
tense or relaxation catching fire earlier in the season,
in the hard-wired ounces of corn-forced yields,
whether swimming in the temporal instantaneous
grain or slow process of being conjoined with glowing
antler branches under Pacific shade, with mammalian
tipping points that cry out on the cutting edge
of 5 a.m., the hurricane eye which naturally selects,
muscling muds where emptiness cooks up
suddenly slow unseasonable stirring Bosch
open-arterial refinery vats, wheeling incomplete
acreage iron-bellied in muds, however
unthinkable the future appears to be looking.

SHE WALKS BETWEEN VILLAGES

Her elephants rumble out their relative positions
      a few octaves down.
Her sun's come through the way wood's shaped
      day after day for years.
Her ancient world has had wide-spread grasses
      growing in a warm wind.
She's familiar with canyons of rain and space
      where box elders branch
over the door where you enter in front of a long wave
      out of the forgotten,
as the cliff edge of the continuum establishes
      the scent of ripe oranges.
Her neocortex is like bread made out of uranium
      and sea lions diving.
Her color tattoo of liberated sexual medicine
      appears on the inner thighs
of a hill where exotic plants stretch up to secluded
      homes like old flames.
She's let her hips roll when entering the hall
      with both hemispheres intact.
She drives on gravity while her subatomic mother
      brushes her long DNA.
Her praying mantis attending the university
      of leaves learns what to do.
She pitches awake on the sea of resemblances
      engendering her capacity
to work over the week and walk between villages
      like an East Indian
sadhu adapting to rigorous conditions on a blue
      planet in the cosmos.

FUTURE PARTS OF THE PAST

The incomprehensible uncompromised business of family,
the nature of unchecked addition, and divisions in identity,
the reversals of bad with good, or falsified high-end propriety,
the risks to a future expecting outages to appear predestined,

the air fighting the sun over what's left for the wild horses,
the common sense going unplugged, sea-soaked or infrared,
the raw volts torn from the violet socket, or however it feels,
the dust and heat as metabolisms speak something missing,
the place human beings weren't the first to be disrupting,

the extraordinary paradox being left behind in progressions,
the vast wheels hauberk of red-eyed star-rimmed unknowns,
the future galaxy in a second with more days than any of us has,
the widening into which we were born in a land tended by bees,

the coordinated sweeps before bees head out, to return with gold,
the mind which is ready, already lit by blossom through the yards,
the cypress-driven interlocking pairs of gyres within the cells,

the purple black eyes of grackles as being grows closer to thought,
the girl who has been holding an acorn, for the feel, she says,
the kelp forest where a manta ray glides in quantum parramatta,
the thought reaching a man's arm, to the hive being protected,
the future place that draws the girl in, the way it reminds her,

the painter with a hat of lit candles facing the ceiling fresco,
the turn-of-the-world Madonna and Child in survival of senses,

the eyes that go back to night, to witness the ways it arrives,
the plumes of untouchable ancient rustling that won't be complete,
reports of Madam David-Neel of powerful earnest contemplators,
the new or old man or woman embarking for the philharmonic futur

INSCRUTABLE NORTHERLY DRIFT

The night and day sky continues to wheel in slow motion of the genome shifting with Celsius north.

At intermixed latitudes, the Pacific sea lions dive in swims beyond littoral brines, suspended in heaves, salt in the mouth of waters, the burn of bees in the forgotten and recollected, the quantum only hour as unfinished as all species.

Voices out of the future come with the rain on back of drought, the inscrutable green where a chance exists, with dusts that fall in lobbies where forests have left their imprint.

Blood breathes out into blood, which breathes out into blood through miles in common, presence of species in common, where the extravagant overpeopling of hectares exists in common, Pacific island torches at the perimeter, the future drifting further north on its hungers.

Unexpected beauty we haven't named will take its time, however long the documentary footage resembles genetic complexity, where a feather can lift into thunderhead multiples and survive in jurisdictions of the unseen.

FLOODING EXPOSURE

The fiery plants powering trunks of red hissing electricity,
the well-oiled condescension behind flood-lit razor wire,

blood-seeing circumstances embraced through a few feathers,

the prehistory along lit edges of the next rain falling to Earth,
churns at the core showing what's making the body round, the
current collaborative release of blossoming plum and hawk,

the humpback whales on polar arcs over thousands miles or so,
the blue-black storm over foothills, the medieval scans of iris,

the drifting swirl of seawater at the drain where centuries may go
unremembered fast, into root-cooled animal-headed antiquity,
grip of a fingerprint whorl within archaic states of fluorescence,

yellow skirts made of bamboo fiber seen from a future collective,
the present existence at the foot of a tree, however much is visible,

the collisions of alertness and breathing in mineral halls of the cells

the past-present Manifest Destiny where seawater screen doors slam
the opposite-talk out of principle discovering itself having been let go
the cunning in an unleashed natatorium of public oversimplification

the swells of oceanic Stravinsky with owl-purred half-absolute floods

EVERYTHING IS WAVES

[waves turn into energy]

At least one-hundred billion
galaxies sweep us along

again showing photographs of the eclipse

of the world's poor
who're hungry

a few sparrows mercy-gripping maples
after flights through tinctures
over the red taverns

as breaking subatomic reception
of the body in each cell

when glaciated time is melting
the ways craving has light

uncertain as a finch's touch
on cheekbones of a model

walking in space made by hips
of a smallest particle

held by the immensity of weight
in unseen circling

however complex breathing can be

however oceanic
and long as scattered sunflowers

or the smallest grip
taking on form
and this burden
undcr daylime stars.

ENTANGLEMENT

Electrical stories blow in from distant civilizations
        and villages at the edge
of time which stops and starts up with every birth
in a surgical theater or rush-hour taxi backseat
        at the midpoint of last century
before the global population tripled. These stories
rake over the small houses in a wing of bone
and confusion of untried chances and private
confessions packed with warnings and reprimands
passed along for generations in anger and love,
        with sensory overload
and deprivation, victorious elation and surrenders,
strategic reprisals and breakthroughs, endeavor
and betrothal, with thick slices of embarrassment
        spiraling up black-red
dust clouds behind massive industrial harvesters
on the horizon with open-pit acreages gone airborne
        alongside chemical debris
from *better living through chemistry* ladled out
through biomaterial flues in the days of much trading
in non-lucid identity and banding together of many
        for expressed prognostications
in hot-tempered providence, with bandying relative
stays and familial armistice, uncanny private
power projects around a hearth or declaration
        of loyalty not open
for debate, out of extraordinarily hungry desire
for recognition or meaning in the province of hours,
where the long dark hair of the mother in Genesis
        still appears, shimmering
from the unfathomable burst into tool-making brain
that must have happened suddenly, over millennia,
        one person to the next,
where complexity triggers more out of faculties
until the renaissance masters in candled hats
are painting angels with faces that resemble ours.

SPRING KICKS IN

City highways take the future
around the bend of the river
of money. Women assume further control.
The next human world aims its nuclear
torpedoes, as transcontinental jets
haunt the place, taking off and landing
on autopilot. Sons decide they're daughters,
while the compass spin undergoes
its heavy journey across the charred
proving grounds of spring. Beetles burrow
into trees high up, where winter ends
and may return less often. Alien weather
balloons crack into a dimensionless chill.
Elk herds edge north, as the north pole
down-drains into newly claimed shipping
lanes. Parabolic receivers scan for eyes
of doubt over ends and their means.
Blue-suited company men gas up directly
removed from undead talk of extinctions.
A long hot kiss familiar with liberated
hip bones wavers before the collapse
of procreative love. Forebears continue
to break up and drift off from work shoes
and overcoats. Habits that grew out of fear
into lifestyles refuse to reveal their North
American arrogance in its rainwater
spend-drift street-carried flatness
under shirts and blank-slate asking
for reassurance around petroglyphs
that dwarf the possible ways to feel.

ERA NOT OF WAR

We've come out of the dust
in our mother tongue
not to praise the people
with astronomical hoards of bucks
and numbers, but those who've risen
out of volcanic ashes, those pushed
into labors for biddings not theirs,
who're capable of envisioning peace
between nations when negotiations
take work with credible research
and willingness to hear clearly,
when missiles fire off at the twitch
of a ring finger. We're here to give
our piece to the masters of war
who may be disinterested in seeing
what's before them, as they duck
responsibility for the consequences
of their acts just to maximize profit.
Every day the masters of war fight
the human consensus, masters who,
stumbling upon disputes, provide
not wisdom but lethal arms to every
side, who in the face of Earth's limits
of materials wage their public war
to control others and gut education.
And yet we're here to recognize
those who've stood for peaceful
coexistence, who understand links
of firing off a missile to destruction
on the ground, who can envision
many years of peace, with altruism
toward those in need, and not forget
that war is a catastrophic collapse.

NOTES ON THE CULTURE

I.

Joe Cocker, wet at the temples, sweat
on his locks, dripping in the fall
of mists at Woodstock, standing square
and rocking, lifting the underneath
self into "A Little Help from My Friends,"
wailing into the mic, planting
paradigm change in the continuum—

II.

The 2014 *Democracy Now* interviews
that laid out a case for taking Gulf War
torture to the international criminal
court for the thirty-nine who were killed
or who "inadvertently died," in the face
of the 25-50% who were innocent,
or in the "wrong place at the wrong
time," the way a colonel put it—

III.

The National Voter Convention at PSU
where an Ohio attorney sold us his book
of legal evidence proving how the right
wing stole the 2004 Ohio Presidential
election, therefore the White House
that Kerry apparently won, with identical
tactics found in other states since then,
and what's changed is the national media
adjusting its story, to ignore it all—

IV.

Eddie Vetter present at the Dylan concert
which was shown on TV, with Eric
Clapton, George Harrison, and you name
them at the intersection of New York
and time, Eddie Vetter bending over
a moment, then standing up into center
mic singing Dylan's "Masters of War,"
exacting tenor, breathtakingly, bringing
the house down to the root of bearing—

HOLE IN MORTALITY

Dr. Jung draws with certainty on his briar pipe.
In a released Latakia licorice puff of smoke,
      he asks, "How do you know you aren't
      already riding on back of the red stallion?"
The magical number exists, in the indivisible.
What to do, what one must do when perceiving
      the next instant keeps the nest open
      to the only sky blue enough to protect it.
"It's possible to not be impressed with advances."
A fox sniffs out the sea floor in rock of the foothills.
Dr. Jung roars with classical silence while he listens.
A lion prowls in the Western mountains unfinished.
"In the nest are the four eggs love has placed."
When sunlight floods the present, color erupts
      out of the primordial periodic table.
"What mortal is prepared to prove a negative?"
"How will you establish you're no Communist?"
A limb of speaking crashes down off the tree,
      blowing a hole to the stone floor
      of the basement under the basement.
Dr. Jung's books glow with eucalyptus incandescence.
In the fiery mandala, the four corners are sacred,
      converged where are, in the center.
"Unconscious cloud cover hangs over the stage
      on which we act many parts."
"Dramas of birth spill off a gargoyle tongue."

LATE

How do you face the fall
of ice as we know it,
the end of a white bear,
and scrawny gray whales,
the shrinking swarms
of plankton with gulleted
bugling elephant great heart
of continents shot point blank,
as the cooking heat sinks south
and drains north, scouring rains,
the piped-up and blasted ancient
sunlight melting ancient ice?
For how do you mourn fire
we can't measure in a finch's wings,
or a dried-out late forest California
tinder flash, sun burning its planets
around on circling magnetic
geo-positional violet landings
through binoculars in the eyes
of a wild deer fly, a green-harvested
hazelnut in the squirrel's warm
mouth, and those millions forced
to migrate from drowning cities
on oceanic coasts of matter,
when we're going to be
gone or possibly still here?

THRESHOLD

Before you go, of course, be sure to open the door.
You can't much step through a stationary front
screen of hermetic hell-fired locomotives blasting
and rumbling in, their twenty long tons groaning
and squealing like bridge steel failing in a quake
when the trains, simultaneously, reach the station.
And yet even if you've passed through the threshold,
you won't enjoy your constitutional if you're swamped
with flooding of your farmlands, whether by seawater
or bituminous heavy oil drilled out of Canada. If so,
you might want to start moving your feet right now,
before present erections include a refinery bolted up
around you with so much momentum you're stuck
working for it twenty-four hours a day, if you prefer
to keep breathing and assimilating your nutrients.
Look, we've reached significant levels of saturation
of people on Earth, a point where one road drops off
to a dead end, you could call it, and only the other,
no longer worshipping fire as a gift given by gods,
could lead to a future humans are able to survive.

THE LOW ROAR OF SEAWATER

Doesn't the rumbling roar of seawater weight
rock day into night, drawing appetite out of depths?
Where earliest survival shaped bones of the torso
out of wild rain and the spectrum, haven't bread
and its absence advanced unfinished history?
Unanswered hunger can make you unknowing,
of course, unable to speak your father's language.
Weight of the hollows heaves up with what weighs
down the forest floors sinking lightning-first in cells.
Wing-beat swells, face-flashes of intuited gravity,
and sublime last principles of wilderness balance
on more remote consequences most of the ancestors
wouldn't have considered. The moment expands
and contracts, a few descendants coming down
the road in this direction, with unpredictable needs
carrying on a mile down in sleep, as living honesty
thickens and the air of this split-second chance
saddens, before we've seen how generous it was.

SHE RINGS UP

She calls you from the future
that continues to be seen
where everyone intersects.
Her willowing has much truck
with civilized yields buoyant
with weight of the people.
Her blue Olympic pools drop
to unknowable depths down
past fluid equivalencies
with understated remorse,
as thermonuclear truce bears
the identity of her processors
in end-of-night rigs hauling
photographs back to immensity.
Her undiluted whole spirals
out of the first eggs delivering
copper condors into the sky
over descendants mollified
by socio-ethical potency.
Her cavernous walls of bison
France flee the single drop
of a catastrophic anvil under
layers of leaves and soils,
armor and bones, bricks and car
wrecks, as she concentrates
lightning-first on cosmic multiples
of Buddha's birth shattering
on contact with transcendental
forests into new Kandinskys
ghost-whipping past ice-cold
garages from when we were little.

MOTHS ON THE FRONT SCREEN

The moths fly after transformation in arms of the plants. Ice melts in terrific splits and the truck of tissue and bone smoldering in wing-beat swells.

Going about business in the mineral summer have been moths tendering the collective.

Through weight and infinitesimal lightness, in the workhorse ancestry of cells, the spectrum's packed into rock of day into night, the low roar of seawater weight asking, *What do you think will last?*

Far from the ocean, early night moths bring quickness to more children, as unmasked as anything is.

The moths land on the front screen between species. A few of the less settled bank off infrared Cheyenne energies, as a few flute silently through chemical mists.

Unclassified Amazon moths will be drying their wings where the next leaves go under.

Couldn't we have stopped at the root of hungers, before willingness to sacrifice the future for a little more now?

Venus in the winds says, *This body floats on origin*. A muskellunge lingers in cold pools at the bottom of water, out of sight but close enough to feel. A door blows open in the atmosphere from the long-term fault of *All this is yours*.

THE LIFE OF LIGHTNING

Lightning's an eruption of light
instantly losing its camouflage.
Left in a long wait for it to slam back
into the doorframe, we're sensing
weight of the world that's collected
maybe over our heads and roiled in
agitations enough to return us
to fundamental bearings of high and low,
cold and hot, here or not with mooling
herds and recent tall drinks of water,
around Eisenhower causeways
and expressed cocoons of mantis
that drip a milk of tiny white baby
praying mantises scrambling over one
another to the ground, where lightning
happens in a lifetime, over a lifetime,
in a hot emanation out of and back
to the origin, embodied as a leap made
from one side of the canyon to the other
as if it were nothing coming from the future
to be part of the present that dwarfs us,
creating a revelation of unthinkable
wiring that pulses in a bolt however much
we believe we've nailed it down, generations
here and gone in a flash of fathomlessness
that occurs to the mind as a background
effect of time, lightning at night throwing
the place into relief showing small yards,
hammered roofs, giving us no choice
but to see what a short life
looks like, drilling the ground
as it leaves the air shimmering
with what remains to be seen.

LITTLE TIME PASSES

A late '60s Beatles album resounds in the front room through all that has happened, the way sun falls in the rain.

Corn under the sun in the summer doctored by bees carries their touch and their longing, where fractals turn out shaping the species as the planet spins and orbits. Case studies piled on old hotel tables darken until boxed and carried off, then reappear decades later in glass hallways where lenses extending perception are being refined.

Ground gives off purple skirts, yellow apples, and Tibetan rings as canopied rain forests sway. The small meeting in the mid-'70s in which Very Venerable Kalu Rinpoche explained, *It is very rare for a being to take human form*, was a few hours ago. Sun arrives in green beans, pasta, and raspberries, in feathers and paper, where we might be pushing 64 though little time has passed.

Moss grows over the unused steps into multiple spreads of plants in a seed. Prismatic readings of fortune fly from the ferns in back, returning to the wilds of abstract expression.

III.

The universe is shaped the way it would sound. This
presentation focuses on an exploration of Sacred Geometry,
Fibonacci ratios and the Laws of Harmonics, beautifully
illuminated and made clear with the performance of music ...
Vibrations cause and are the reason for the Fibonacci ratios –
shapes we find in parts of our bodies, in seashells, galaxies,
crystals, sunflowers, orbits, eggs, buds, pines cones and in
the unfolding of embryonic life. — **Lorin Hollander**

THE WINDS RAKE THROUGH

The winds sweep in from early music conservatories,
while the offshore churns are forever scouring out
their cooking pots. Gusts spike around the extravagant
and frugal, where riverous forces split, splashing wildly
through the millennia that the flicker woodpeckers
hammer back together. As higher inclinations smolder,
both cold and hot exacerbate in slow motion, hundreds
of years rifling through cathedrals of firs, in rock-bottom
shuck of each leopard layer going back to the mother.

———————

Every cell alive selects what's staying and goes ahead
to negotiate with officials with a direct line on supplies.
Each keeps abreast of the news in heart-beat oneness.
Every cell cooks on its iron stove an elaborate next meal
and is engaged in major undertakings that surround it
with weather and complex communications that pertain
to its abilities, whether dusk bleeds through from new
feedlot antibiotics and hormones, or reflective shields
guard the Rhone glacier, or 300' wind turbines revolve
around stuck Yankee ambivalence in the heartland.

———————

Don't the animals cry and sing for cells
under the moon and the sun, lowing
and bellowing, calling and chuckling,
growling with diplomacy and paratactic
urgency, projecting their lines of sight
and their voices? When flat on your back
from your overcome animal body, will you
swallow your medicine? Will you drink
through a glass straw? So do you favor
resuscitation by extraordinary means?
Can what's happening be crowding in
around you, the way people have been
the animals, when who among us knows
where the time goes off in its old Desoto?

———————

There we are, racing largely well-fed
forward, as dusk settles into slipstream
spreads, as it lunges, salt-sea bulk going
fast forward, pursuing instantaneous mute
in rushing Arctic roar that intrudes on board
rooms from rifled-up all-you-can-own sea
floods swelling the dollar. With coastal caves,
compass arcs, brackish whirlpool vexations
foaming in urchiny spits with truck-wrecked
milks and prayerful craving all muled-up,
unstoppable global impregnation peaks.

———————

Sunburst cellular acuity lifts from the root
of inception, as willowing shares of lightness
reach through the nutrient chain-mandala
into swaying slow shoulders of a she-elephant
from the centers of future speech. Observed
may be landslides of hunger looking for reasons,
boa-constricted boughs of reclining bobcats,
a few mammoth tangles of disemboweled seat
springs, where forebears co-create what's seen
of the spectrum, with cries for warm shelter
of the mother, cries invented out of urgency
or shock at the beginnings of consciousness
arriving from back in matter older than soup
and bowls, before the oil-lamp whales dropped
to unknowable depth in unsettled scarlet dark.
So the brain guards the mind it considers
its apprentice, as the body experiences being
as if entering the garden which has grown it
out of much more than the mind can take in.

———————

The spired nucleus sprouts. The seed for a tree
rests on its limbs. The tree exists in the seed.
Waves happen to spread through the sycamore
leaves. Transcendental soils carry mushroom-fed
sequoia in crystallographic sharpening, shuddering

night as a moth flies into future impoverished rooms.
Vast clocks of the Arctic bleed out along miles-long
stretches of socioeconomic tree line not about to fall.
Delicate clusters of spiny eggs stick to blind surgery
of saltwaters, the moon with its pendulum pounding
the coast, erasing more future from its animal past.

———————

The complex cosmic array
in the uncovered night sky
is evidence of a reverberating
string at the bottom of matter.
The Stradivarius of Valeriy Sokolov
is evidence of neural urgency
that over time fills with devotion
and supersedes the alternatives.
Spreads of cosmos, 360° by 360°,
surround Beethoven late quartets
present before understanding,
and make each move of cells
in the liquid atmosphere within
the mother. As galaxies whisper
and groan, the night sky embraces
sleep behind evidence of lightning
in the guitar of Eric Clapton.

IN THE MORNING

Nothing lives that hasn't grown
or yielded to effects of time
or depended on primary health
of the surroundings, on balance
in the interlinked animals and plants,
the visible and microscopic symbiosis,
where nothing grows that isn't cells,
that doesn't change or fall
within the laws of matter,
as the sun creates what has legs,
what burns away, or swims in a drop
of water, or sings from a branch
in the morning, as the sun makes mind
possible where light breaks open
into being and nothing lives
that hasn't changed or been changing
while this galaxy alone saucers
with hundreds of billions of suns,
given what we can see from here
where nothing lives outside being
and it's easier not to think
about reports of a sixth extinction
than to imagine runaway climate
disruption mostly caused by us
or to realize that this life must end.

WITH STILLNESS IN TREES

I.

The instant this is begins timeless,
at the origin, before it compresses
into the genome, as the compass flies
and time lasts past counting. Distances
between us converge when a gull, crying
out, calls for cells in solidarity with gulls
that emerge in the instant as individuals,
tree trunks drawing out into space
with green leaves tracking the sun
at angles of cosmic rays, from surfaces
of their water into calving winds,
through pitches of vibration in neural
spectra with elevated *gravitas*
in which no numbers stand
for the heaviness of starlight.

II.

The instant concentrates timeless lasting
that ends in great sunflower Van Gogh
fields bathed in sun, wheat turned gold
while the crow flies, over public doing
that at first would have resembled love
or giving night back to day, the way blue
in the sky has been filled with Beethoven,
very venerable quiet Buddha, and Momma
Mia renunciation sweeter than weeks loose
as years under spiral galaxies Van Gogh saw
reaching out of the genome sweet as Miles
Davis holding a blue pitch close to the wall,
no matter the jibber-jabber, with Willie Mays
the exquisite gloveman covering center,
knocker of the skin off the ball, who showed
how to move beyond your century and yet
stay within it, whoever pushes accelerators.

INSTINCT

This time the ancients within us seem to be wrong,
firing missiles to stop war, assisting billionaires
to help the economy, declaring environmentalists
extremists and spying on them, animals setting up
shop further north the more global Celsius we have.
Cellular ancestors within us have their hands full
with basic hot and cold, as the psyche practices,
leaving a wake of latent photochemical reciprocity
between long falls of rain and pulsatile solar waves.
Effortless heart-beat simulations deliver the instant,
oyster-lit, the wild sweet Sitka unfinished spruce,
state-of-the-art silences under star-clustered night
from before birth advanced symmetry 360° around,
the glow in edible leaves and archaic spinal centering.
The rare birth you were ready to inhabit in your time
resounds and splashes with overflow rain and sun
in the hour stopped in a burst of current indwelling
microorganisms resonating a whisper of great power.

SAYINGS THAT SLOWLY DISSOLVE

Loss and blowing sea-salt winds reach the immense future
energy turbines powering further birth.

Connections that the cells built into the brain correspond
with complexities of the surroundings.

The body expects future meaning to occur in the present.

Powered with autonomous inhalation and release, the brain
leans on trees and burning riddles of coal.

Planetary oceans slowly dissolve parts of the sky, even times
of birth-trauma guilt or Stradivarius joy.

Heavy Indonesian rainstorms have little option but to cash in
on the more unaccommodated species.

And what are the Siberian tigers doing, making appearances
as lost ghosts in tropical rainforests?

PLACE IN THE SAUCERING GALAXY

Where every cell's tied to what hopes in a molecule

where every move appears to be taking it out on the wild,

where the borax of wisdom bites at your aging boot heels
behind red velvet curtains in the embassy of opposites,

the baroque current wheeling through air and the sea
electromagnetic and precise as archaic and modern as skin

with preachers predicting the absolute end of thinking

hypnotized anger going about bamboozling political will,

the coast of all morning that sinks its silver spoon into the roar
glistering an apparatus squealing with 18th century assumptions

where inflations of rain feather off the overflow of desire,
where the exact day and hour will kick in after us,

tongues touching as small animals from before word

where light shatters in parallel prisming with mind,
as the clear threat to the population is the population,

old firs risking their limbs all night through the day,

all that exists playing keyboards of the genome without asking
where the unmanageable era crows in displays of impermanence

with the future laying leathery eggs in a pit on the beach.

RESILIENCE OF THE MASSES

For we will survive with a resistance of spectacular color in the provinces of parrots and electrical washes across sides of cuttlefish talking in displays to the living eye, in light of the buoyant intracellular sun. We will find our way past any unschooled disavowal plummeting out of agrarian dance gone sour before sorrowful high-caliber erosions walking on borrowed bones under rhino-gray camouflage.

On the rising oceans of microorganisms, we'll see what's thrived or fallen in inexplicable pin-drop struggles, with or without more libraries cabbaged by fumy reserves of money-grabbing poachers who, no matter what, charge on, unleashing eruptions of reinvented gases that evade Teutonic regulation. But we will be following the road that no doubt leads out of here, making the place more sane.

For we will be leaving hermetic Chryslers and the muffled foul dirges of combustion. Our searchlights scouring unconscious Mariana trenches, our resistance panthery and lucid, we'll design tantric armistice on rises. For soon enough, salt-sea spawns will be flooding anyone's buried offshore vaults. As the root sinks, we will resist unspooled polarizations unleashed on persons. We will stand alert, in places possibly far from enthusiasm or solitude. We will not surrender bell-raked and ringing on archaic grounds to freefall baptisms or fundamental transplantations.

For we will harness current billionaire hoarding for the public work ox it is. We will intervene to bar further snake-tongued licks of metal-mongering predations from holding neighborhoods hostage. We will keep finding the route and adhere to fact until heavy money stops abandoning communities and damages are reversed.

MUSHROOM REVERBERATION

Into the cloud-lit fall of leaves, slate-white heads crown smooth in the grasses before opening their turbans in melts of air.

Slippery with bark dusts and dew, pale fruits of the underground continue to show up faceless, but not without sense in the cells.

Mushrooms roil, bursting out of node into the atmosphere taking on spores for lamp-quick expansions arterial with spawns and fractal spirals, as feather out through urban heat and falls of rain.

Breakthroughs on the ground can appear between sleep and waking, as morning concentrates under shape of the body any remains of unhouseled night.

Between turgid shank and yoni cradling her baby, come moss-quiet yields with sweltering build from below. What gathers releases, echoing in the trunk, into limbs, drawn by smallest translucent threads over miles, where mineral transit goes.

Root sense rises, sinking with core-spun multitudes fir forests have had in a snake roar.

SAYINGS AS THEY OVERFLOW

I.
The worlds that sunflowers open
will be overflowing on Earth
as it reaches velocity in time.

II.
Flames may have started then stopped
at the stone core in an instant part
of the ambient Big Bang echoing *om*.

III.
Back-country great horned owls have bursts
with blank dark extractions flying ahead,
and ride on shoulders that found a backbone.

IV.
As anything known approaches
infinity, it's already been
the plants feeding on light.

V.
Taking a step carries along the past parents of parents,
parents of distant parents, back to more people alive
than were counted for the medieval European census.

VI.
A North Atlantic right whale
will inhale with the great
lungs of an ancient Celtic arena.

VII.
The exquisite Gorge will have waterfalls
split by a drop of sudden rain
recovering in a Stonehenge of rain.

VIII.
Even a loose sprout driven by the current
appears to have old salmon shadows
thrown onto many east county porches.

WINGS LIFTING THAT FALL

I.

The wings lifting that fall in thermals and arcing heaves,
single hours of sky that avalanche in streaming light
from mesas and peaks to the heart of matter and chance,

II.

the seen and unseen heights that garden facts on the ground
for the mind falls with sunlight lifting in wings that thicken
with precision between openness and shuddering propulsion

III.

through the genome of forgiveness for whatever failed to work
or became epidemic, fogged out, or what opened and spread
along impulse before drawing back, retracting into a landing,

IV.

for the current seven billion will sleep and then wake, sleep
then wake, each birth into longing that begins in the cells
where it ends, as light and dark will swallow what happens

V.

with what never came to be, living sunlight that has let us
witness through lapses and stands what balances inside
its bearings, where palaces have been built out of capability

VI.

and stay maybe a handful of years before what was forgotten,
unknown, or far from sync bears down, the wings morning
and evening taking the current light into long-term alignment

VII.

of the instrument of adaptation, the adjustment of intensity
to cellular discovery that goes on beneath this lifetime,
in the practice of intrinsic worth of the interlinked species.

EYE OF THE SPIRAL

The carrying capacity of Earth
exists in a bubble of gambling.
At risk have been descendants,
while old assumptions barley
with vulnerable wingspan paths
from birth, around marigold
scent and pungency of intelligence
in modulated rings around core
tendering the subconscious roar
of the oil lantern self that walks
on eggshell digs past anthropological
cracks in uses of photographic eyes.
So the tremulous intones. Slow-motion
acts burn through the shock-sleeping
taps of synaptic occupying forces
on untested quantum subcontinents.
So complexity arcs over on meridians
where the world has been nothing
if not this moment, this sense
of the whole where the wind comes
flying at your back into your animal
evolution, its sunburst swells
fired up with genetic immensity.
So urgency invents a crystalline
claw licked into acts by rattlesnake
tongue in the coliseum of the old
religion ringing disruptive bells
packed ten feet down with cellular
clay at the funeral of people
in the future, where it turns out
you can have too many people.

from **Double Helix**

"It is raining DNA outside. On the bank of the Oxford canal at the bottom of my garden is a large willow tree, and it is pumping downy seeds into the air. ... [spreading] DNA whose coded characters spell out specific instructions for building willow trees that will shed a new generation of downy seeds. ... It is raining instructions out there; it's raining programs; it's raining tree-growing, fluff-spreading, algorithms. That is not a metaphor, it is the plain truth. It couldn't be any plainer if it were raining floppy discs." **— Richard Dawkins**

✳

The properties of molecules
have them moving,
snapping into Indonesian peat forests,

locking them into machinery of dragonflies
in a gnat's eyes, one with another,
one joining the next, one life to the next
one life. They never stop swimming

out on their fins, going off on hyena hunts,
grains pouring, dunes roiling at the foot
of water, sloping carbons through overhead
vocabularies that turn into western rain,

mineral infinitesimal dusts that pepper the lips
and working tongues, drawn as inclination is
to centers of solidity, of something over nothing.

As fir trees in their up-roar from the origin
donate all they've been to the present,
roots send up their green flames
as cells stretch, shaping reach in the compound
complex instant, symbiotic cells deciding
in flux, buffering adrenaline spikes
and ontological stews.
                    They appear unable to stop
reaching out in organic symmetry, letting mind emerge
not from an exact location in the brain,
but through spontaneous overflow of all parts.

Continually out of compass core, biochemical
matter's vibratory and concentrated,
tended by transpolar circulation of oceans,
warmed by transmutations, the cells

carrying us and sharing these eyes
where we're taking them in the world.

✺

Lost to us, of course, have been large numbers
of visions the unconscious delivered
in esoteric breakthroughs,

including operatic tenor declarations of divine intervention
accompanied by exhortations of ordinance
as prevail over antithetical trajectories,

raving and ravenous anti-material rock-erupted looming
spontaneous combustions of prehistoric ochre
grass-brushed cave-wall mergings
in the heart-beat public drum,

with delirious dehydrated visitations of unvoiced bounty
achieved through fever-spelled visitation
of out-gardened fertility in a time of scarcity,

back-channeled final cautionary fragments in a forest necklace
that broadcasts a virgin protectorate,

ripe dusk-soaked blood-seeing scans with sharp viscera
linked to kindred evolutionary perception,

mushrooming under-the-ground revelations of the undivided
origin of one then one then one and others
with harped-up talks of moving waters,
lectures of bark, and abstract-thinking ants,

or praying-mantis liberation as results in tales of being
beset by giant battalion-beetle mandibles through
which one nevertheless passes,

near-drownings in which mythical feminine presence
gave breath from the cosmic breast
to cataplectic spells of pickerel heads
at the end of the lion-clawed periodic table,

stertorous moments in which a starling speaks
      prognostic Latin chronicles
      in pedagogical quicksilver outline,

terrifying late-evening shadow sightings
      of the acrimonious newly buried en mass,

automatically written transcriptions of the esemplastic fringe
      integrated into aesthetic manifestoes
      transmitted person to person by teleportation,

sudden hurls made by an unknown bodily guest who unifies
      power with reception at the point of penetration,

poulticed agony-fueled out-of-the-body extemporal journeys
      to unconquered terrain where new cures glow
      behind latent stands of teleological old-growth,

inspired communal lapses into an unstudied less-modulated
      tonic tongue for the glory of profound bearings
      originated by shock over inexplicable goings-on,

quasi-spatial levitation in a diamond bloom on the blue calm
      of honesty in concentric rings of allies
      and detractors maintained in abeyance,

trunk-shuddering hallucinatory spreads of psychic songbirds
      delivered beyond question by bolts
      in the mycelial underground,

with grandfathered-in clavichord churned out
      by friction of the spheres
      for the delight of lovers and lambs.

✳

Each place we've taken in
we're looking from,
as through purple-black eyes
of grackles or multiples
of off-split sumacs of the whole

arterial crimson branching spreads
through the meeting chambers
open to anyone who's never seen

pronghorn antelope racing across
foothills as to anyone who never
has stopped to ponder photographs
of the Sombrero galaxy or Messier 104
taken from the Hubble orbiting

each cell watching from the mind
of its own, from before symbiosis grew

into a spread-wing lichen moth
for anyone entering the emergency
room stalls where they'd be falling
into a range of personal transience

as cross-sectioned as these hours
arriving from abstract First Avenue
are being painted expressionistic
by infinity all night as the truly old

goats of white ice have a go
along throat-edges of the next

hand-cut diamonds melting
one week, then Great Lakes
wall-eyed pickerel flying off
to Canadian waters the next,

given the build-up of summer
in lower regions of heating
and following one's only social

responsibilities of thirst, hunger,
shelter, desire, giving to what was
known once to be straight-ahead
organic truth over the unraked

months of plankton-eating
that reach us each moment
a hydromedusa jellyfish, lit
from within like a Pacific city,
parachutes through the whole

ancient carnival in the subliminal
homes and symmetry of eyes
the intelligence of the cells has
employed, in accord with its own

longer-term primordial hatchings
and rarest of mammalian births.

✸

The paradise of badgers may never be reconciled.

A frog without resources is in a world of trouble.
A diamond will have been cut with sufferings,
both the unknown and known.

Frogs with extra appendages have been savored by herons.

The sphinx was erected by luminous dancing women
in an attempt to protect the old bags of bones with money.

The cross appeared after the pope and the bishop made it.

Lonely beds of roses were never comfortable.
The combustion engine has burned the masses.

Newts take off their masks after they appear.

Just one pipe of a warmed-up cycle can make you shout.

The pyramids were erected by luminous dancing women
whose phones were tapped after they covered them with gold.

Pi will not stop until numbers are gone.

To hell with consequences,
astronomical money will do anything, anything.

Extra paradise continues to be promised
to anyone with exceptionally big money.

A diamond can pass through a badger.
The lake may not believe this or anything you tell it
if you don't pay the price.

So the sphinx was given a fierce inscrutability
of man-sized vaults in waves of the motionless sea.

✸

A swing of cycles at the root
of heat and bearings
on the ground, the coyote
circling back behind the languages
of species,
            the overpour
arcing solid blue at the beginnings
of contemplation within filtering
membranous bioswales of psyche,

the ladling out of unfolding spiral
genome that settles down into cells,

the parallel chambers of cello,
Bach crackling with integrity
in the evolution undergone
by a womb-walled fetus, the falling lift

that fills the simple rounding-off
of apple, conscious sense of mother
in the collective body of rain,

the Bartok shadow thrown off
by flames of abstract winds,
blue concentration that rises
to rooms buoyant over sea-level,

a chickadee in C-sharp threading
her flight in between stone
going back to fresh anonymity,
her curve in the pull
or draw of prismed sound.

❉

The ancestral invention of singing with inarguable voice in sync
the brain that works on more than it cares to release to the mind,

the present altered through hearing it turn into recognized form,
the red-hot flats from the bottom of photochemical scarlet dark,
the rake of splintered Rothko red-violet reds through the chords,

foundational solar nighttime in what has been unattempted doubt,
with drawbacks and an opposite-pulse inherited from the unknown,

light pouring through circulation down to the root of electric nerve,
quick sweeps of withheld recalcitrance waging restraint on *yes* or *no*
the long brick ovens of neo-primitive winter within fits of beseeming,

with tortoise-crawl scrafing howls of antiquity that unhatch in clay,
from plum-wrestled immensity of train bursts within cellular growth

metropolitan labors of infinity with a shadow of unequal distribution
whatever may have been savored or not in the lift unfolding leaves,
the chance to live out the spin of vulnerability and mineral intensity

the sea-bellowing blameless wind of many simultaneous bodies asleep
the capacity of human appetites to face philosophic next generations
with catalyzed uptown discontinuum under million MPH solar waves

within long-term collaborative overflow in the presence of a future
and what may have been in sight, but lacking a name went unseen.

✸

This rain wasn't so long ago
the rock of the coast, saltwater flux

reaching and leaving the visible world
with its breathing sea lion pups,
its raspberry gatherers, as each wave
is a generation passing through blood

of the nearby cattle and young farm Collie,

before leaving its jungle of crucifixes along the road,

the Collie barking at whatever moves past in history
mostly unnoticed, at the edge of this age
which is towering with undiscovered resources

and seaside houses people might long for,
where they'll return and be assured
that they don't need to keep up the labor,
when what number may be able to escape
their own future extinction

as the disparate grasses interweave
through waves of water and light

where the sun's stopped being the holy father

for people calling wherever they are everything they have
and whatever they've seen all there is to be found

as short as these lives are,
as petroglyphic as the writing is
in the shade and bark of trees.

✸

The road knows where it was built to go,
the unclear suffrage of sentient beings,
the contingent aesthetic lulls
and breaking pitch, the long-cradled
genetic hemispheres cross-pollinating,

the museum of stone and unraveling,
for what seems to know in between spores
carried by winds over the beluga ocean,
the onion-peeling Stonehenge of sensorium,

with drives of the defenders of seraphim,
the onset of obscure psychological fibrillation,
the flux of governing obscuration and realisms
with windows that open to melting glaciers,

for this is the urgent present where the future is
growing heaviness that descends on us now
with the red tape of newborn steadiness,
chests of Buddhists that rise and fall with breath
of the high and low Calvinist confirmations
depending on more than the collective notices,

the seahorse carried in the sacred pouch
of the father, revolutions of the unfallen
and peaking burn of art, concert trumpets
that fill their share of lips with blood, Western
hemlock sprawls of rain with its muskellunge
fluid time, for this is the place where the future
endows meanings that are parts of what we do,

the multiple possible hours and severe intelligence
in deep pools, the goose-V independence
and labors of non-stop clock, the Steller's jay
that springs from a branch outside the kitchen,

where the ground of the present we go by ends up
beyond sensation, far beyond any lickety-split
materialism, for being isn't an isolated experience
of consuming a slice of great grandmother's pie,

where leaf-green aphids will be milked by ants
and loyalty's found swigging from the same
jug, the long note saddening without vibrato,

the abdominal lulls of conundrum, afternoon rain
steaming off streets where the present consists
of improvisation and instincts, the consequences
of acts returning to look into the human face
through these eyes, effects with long-standing
residency in these rooms from which they're not
about to move, not now when how much is known

where anything lives, surrounded by everything
made by the living arts of cells, with human
wheel-making that takes orders from the future,
while the road's glowing from the small temples
of roadside apples, where a person won't love
with only one flower, who's swayed on a bridge
over time or driven a truck at the crossroads,

when this is the present on which the future rises
and falls with every small thing that adds up
to what's done, which is the lesson of being
on the road, as somebody here whose selves add up

to one, whose brain holds more than she sees,
whose blossoming squash in the garden will show
when the time's right, whether shafts of dust
are doctoring the roar that rakes through particles
of doubt, where the lightning grains burn fuels

with risks to those they serve, people holding
onto a few coins in purses, who're followed
by scents of baking breads, who work hard
from the root and stand where the next place
is being made by the sun no one will own.

Acknowledgements – Eye of the Spiral

The author gratefully acknowledges publications in which these poems and prose poems originally appeared (at times in other form):

The Bitter Oleander (US): "Sayings as They Overflow"
Bridge (US): "Hole in Mortality"
The Buddhist Poetry Review (US): "Little Time Passes"
Burningword Literary Journal (US): "Era Not of War" & "Spring Kicks In"
Caliban Online (US): "The ancestral invention" (as "The Overflow Present"), "Entanglement," "Eye of the Spiral," "Fluid Rips in the Fabric," "Future Parts of the Past," "Hieronymus Bosch Rings the Caldron Bell," "However Many," "In the Glow of the River," "Lost to us," "Mushroom Reverberatum," "Resilience of the Masses," "She Expands and Contracts with Consciousness," "She Rings Up," "This," "We're looking at light of rain forest moss" (as "Spiraling Chord"), & "The Winds Rake Through"
Calliope (US): "The Low Roar of Seawater"
The Chariton Review (US): "This rain wasn't so long ago" & "What has already broken"
Cold Mountain Review (US): "In the Morning"
Elohi Gadugi (US): "The properties of molecules"
Eunoia Review: "Sayings That Slowly Dissolve"
Fredericksburg Literary and Arts Review (US): "Irreversible Sense"
Ginosko (US): "She Walks Between Villages" & "Threshold"
Hamilton Stone Review (US): "Everything Is Waves," "Possibility at the end," & "The road knows where it was built to go"
Harbinger Asylum (US): "Where the Next Wave Has Been"
Interim (US): "Out of the Quick"
Into the Void (Canada): "Notes on the Culture"
The Kerf (US): "An Ant's Duty," "Blue Scarf" & "Good reasons exist" (as "Scent of the Evening Air")
The Laurel Review (US): "We Must Adapt"
Miramar (US): "Instinct"
Not Your Mother's Breast Milk (US): "A Char Scent in the Air" & "Around Light"
The Oxonian Review (UK): "While the lengthy faithful"
The Pedestal: "Each place we've taken in" (as "Animal Sync")
Plumwood Mountain (Australia): "Wings Lifting That Fall"
Poesy (US): "Before bugling"
Poetry Salzburg Review (Austria): "A swing of cycles at the root" (as "A Chant: Converging in the Air") & "However Many"
Poets Reading the News (US): "The Brain Takes Its Time"
Quiddity (US): "At the Root of Nerve"

ReDactions (US): "Astrologia," "Strings that continue," & "With Stillness in Trees"
Sequestrum (US): "The Life of Lightning"
Shenandoah (US): "The paradise of badgers"
Skidrow Penthouse (US): "Underground pressures"
South Dakota Review (US): "Late"
Stand (UK): "Flooding Exposure"
Toe Good (US): "Out of the Green"
Verse Daily (US): "Astrologia"
Verse News (US): "Encircling Loom"
Weber: The Contemporary West (US): "Inscrutable Northerly Drift" & "Where All Morning the Climate Increasingly Turns"
Wilderness House Literary Review (US): "Place in the Saucering Galaxy"
Wordcraft of Oregon: reprinted with gratitude from *Sea-Level Nerve, Book I* (2014): "A Dream of the Hippos," "Blue Scarf," "Little Time Passes," & "Mushroom Reverberatum" – from Book II (2015): "Encircling Loom," "Inscrutable Northerly Drift," "Moths on the Front Screen," "We Must Adapt," & "Where All Morning the Climate Increasingly Turns"

The author wishes to express appreciation and gratitude for
L. Bernstein, W. Marsalis, R. Shankar, & A.A. Khan; to V.
Van Gogh, W. Kandinsky, M. Rothko, & M. Chagall; to B.
Dylan, N. Young, J. Mitchell, & Lennon & McCartney; to G.
Kinnell, G. Snyder, R. Bly, & P. Neruda; to W. Whitman.
R.W. Emerson, & T.S. Eliot; to D. Raphael, B. Tremblay, C.
Howell, D. Sheffield, H. McCord, L. Smith, B. Mohr, J.
Tipton, J. Otto, D. Memmott, M. Schumacher, & B.
Witherup; to P. Petersen, D. Averill, V. Orr, & B. Siverly; to
J. Bradley, R. Gonzalez, G. Kalamaras, P. Woods, L. & J.
Zimmerman, & Leon; to J. Kaady, J. Sherard, W. Carlile, &
M. Nelson. And most of all to M. Burki – for unending
encouragement, engagement, and love of the arts & other
species.

James Grabill's work appears in Caliban, Harvard Review, Terrain, Mobius, Shenandoah, Seattle Review, Stand, *and many others. Books: four from Lynx House Press,* <u>*Sea-Level Nerve: I & II*</u> *(2014 & 2015, Wordcraft of OR), Branches Shaken by Light & Reverberations of the Genome (2020 & 2021, Cyberwit, India). For years, he taught writing and global issues relative to sustainability.*

Books by James Grabill

Reverberation of the Genome (poems) Cyberwit, 2021

Eye of the Spiral (poems) UnCollected Press, 2021

Branches Shaken by Light (poems) Cyberwit, 2020

Sea-Level Nerve, Book Two (prose poems)
    Wordcraft of Oregon, 2015

Sea-Level Nerve, Book One (prose poems)
    Wordcraft of Oregon, 2014

October Wind (poems) Sage Hill Press, 2006

Finding the Top of the Sky (creative nonfiction with poems)
    Lost Horse Press, 2005

An Indigo Scent after Rain (poems) Lynx House Press, 2003

Lame Duck Eternity (wild poems) 26 Books chapbook, 2000

Listening to the Leaves Form (poems and prose poems)
    Lynx House Press, 1997

Through the Green Fire (creative nonfiction with poems)
    Holy Cow! Press, 1995

Poem Rising Out of the Earth and Standing Up in Someone (poem
    Lynx House Press, 1994 (Oregon Book Award, 1995)

In the Coiled Light (poems) NRG chapbook, 1985

To Other Beings (poems) Lynx House Press, 1981

Clouds Blowing Away (poems) Seizure and kayak Press, 1976

One River (a reverie of poems) Momentum Press, 1975

on Being Within Being

James Grabill's "Being Within Being" reminds us that the "conscious mind [is] still under construction." In these brilliant poems he accelerates our co-evolution with all other creatures, enabling our dive into the living soup of eons, where we can share in the physicality of all life that has ever existed. Grabill's lyricism is extraordinary; it surrounds us with a massive resonance, lifts us up into the great holy of totality.

> — **Lawrence Smith**, editor of *Caliban*; author of novels *Annie's Soup Kitchen* and *The Map of Who We Are* (Oklahoma UP, 2003 and 1997), *The Plain Talk of the Dead,* poems (Montparnasse Ed.), and four books of translation

on *Out of Unfathomable Time*

Like Walt Whitman, James Grabill contains multitudes. I envision him clothed in satellite pictures of a benign, multi-climate reserve where every living being shows up, unconsciously blossoming our language, imaginations and hearts. "The brain loves its many animals." The poems in *Out of Unfathomable Time* are rivers that various beings, events and emotions keep breaking the surface of, rivers that are circular webs pulsing with jazz. So much beauty and wonder here.

> – **Dan Raphael**, poet, performer, editor and reading host, author of 20 volumes of poetry including forthcoming M*anything* (Fall '19)

Responses to *Sea-Level Nerve (Book I)*

[In order of what seems to me to be importance, in terms of establishing credibility and/or of reaching out to potential readers, with the most important first.]

James Grabill has always been at the forefront of ecologically concerned poets, finding the information we need, and speaking as a steward for the natural world. In "Living with the Stern Review" he says, "Even a gnat's dust plants a seed and takes back life." And then he warns us: "What our ancestors believed was endless has come circling back around us."

> — **Allan Cooper**, editor of poetry magazine *Germination;* author of *Gabriel's Wing* and other books of poetry; composer and performer in the band Rosedale

In SEA-LEVEL NERVE James Grabill takes the micro and macro observations of science--in other words, every being and phenomenon in the universe--and pulls them together into a great vision. His unique lyricism is one of the brilliant lights of contemporary American poetry.

> — **Lawrence Smith**, editor of *Caliban*; author of novels *Annie's*
Soup Kitchen and *The Map of Who We Are* (Oklahoma UP, 2003 and 1997), *The Plain Talk of the Dead,* poems (Montparnasse Ed.),
and four books of translation

In **Sea Level Nerve I,** James Grabill has juxtaposed an incredible ecological knowledge-base with a humanizing imagination inside the rolling cadences of spectacular prose poems to expand the powers of human expression through language to pin neurological cell pattern-firings with all they can process into a web of language that synthesizes "a billion respirations" within the living bodies of all botanical and zoological species, their experiences, and the "vastness of the night sky," so that each prose poem builds an enriched context that literally "blows the mind."

> — **Bill Tremblay**, author of *Magician's Hat, The June Rise, Rainstorm over the Alphabet,* and other books, founding editor of *the Colorado Review*

Lyric, vast in scope, replete with riffs both surreal and scientific, James Grabill's prose poems are startling, exhilarating, and profoundly cautionary. Each is an "open-source momentum" propelling us toward a deeper awareness of the rest of this world, a deeper realization of the irreparable changes we humans are bringing to this universe. Each Grabill poem speaks to us as culpable, yet capable of acting responsibly. Each compels us to listen to the part of ourselves most connected to everything else— that timeless place "...within ancient parts of the brain where trees that once saved us come with us."

> — **Paulann Petersen**, Oregon Poet Laureate Emerita, author of *Understory* (Lost Horse P, 2013) and other books of poetry

James Grabill gives a heft of heart to the oft-heard "No One Lives Alone." These proses feel their poetic ways across complex interstices and deep into our human circuitry, which is so profoundly wired into the natural world. Through these explorations of various co-existences, as science meets poetry, sparks fly—beautiful and beguiling.

— **Nance Van Winckel**, Author of Pacific Walkers, NoStarling, and other books of poetry and fiction

One always knows where Jim Grabill stands when time's spent with his poems. *Sea-Level Nerve* is no exception. Everything pours through the poet in these poems; from the cost of mountain waters to the disruptive perception caused by our violent cities. These poems explore each and every sequence of those overlapping realities. Each poem learns where it will go as it goes, and yet for us it's only a matter of simple trust when we drop everything, pick up a walking stick and start tramping with this fine poet/explorer through life's deepest though often unseen and unappreciated movements.

— **Paul B. Roth**, editor of The Bitter Oleander, author of Cadenzas by Needlelight, Fields Below Zero, and other books of Poetry

www.ingramcontent.com/pod-product-compliance
Lightning Source LLC
Chambersburg PA
CBHW071237090426
42736CB00014B/3116